Guide to the New Age

Searching for Self
and
Ancient Wisdom for
the 21st Century

By Heather Piper

Copyright © 2022 Heather Piper

All rights reserved.

ISBN:978-0-6487761-7-8

First published by Heather Piper 2022

The right of Heather Piper to be identified as the Author of this work has been asserted by her in accordance with the Copyright, Design and Patents Act 1988.

All rights reserved. No part of this publication may be reproduced, stored or introduced into a retrieval system, or transmitted in any form, or by any means (electronic, mechanical, photocopying, recording or otherwise) without the prior written permission of the Author.

Any person who does any unauthorized act in relation to this publication may be liable to criminal prosecution and civil claims for damages.

This book is sold subject to the condition that it shall not, by any way of trade or otherwise be lent, re-sold, hired out, or otherwise circulated without the author's prior consent in any form of binding or cover other than that in which it is published and without a similar condition including this condition being imposed on the subsequent purchaser.

DEDICATION

I would like to thank all the teachers I have had over the several decades I have survived within this lifetime for the knowledge they have given to me. Many of these teachers will never know my name and many have left this life a very long time ago. There is so much to learn and so many teachers that it is impossible to name them. To the ancient ones who worshiped nature and the modern teachers who have shown me how to use this wisdom in my own life I thank you all.

My thanks always to my husband Rob who has listened to so many of my ideas with patience and given some very good advice and support during brain drains and frustration.

ACKNOWLEDGMENTS

I have gleaned so much information over so many decades that it is difficult to acknowledge everyone. So I will acknowledge the teachers and providers that have taken part. I also give thanks to the Universe for it's part in all of this.

CONTENTS

	PROLOGUE	i
1	SEARCHING FOR SELF	Pg 1
2	BODY BEAUTIFUL - BODY HEALTHY	Pg 23
3	SO YOU THINK YOU'RE GETTING OLD	Pg 31
4	GARDENING AS THERAPY AND/OR MEDITATION	Pg 41
5	YOU – THE NICE PERSON	Pg 51
6	ANCIENT WISDOM FOR THE 21ST CENTURY	Pg 59
7	ENTERING THE "NEW AGE"	Pg 60
8	NATURAL THERAPIES AND OTHER HEALING MODALITIES	Pg 65
9	THE ANSWER MY FRIEND IS WRITTEN IN THE STARS	Pg 99
	SPIRITS, SPIRITUALITY & SPOOKS	
10	LEARNING MORE	Pg 141

PROLOGUE

In a world where we are told anything is possible it can be a very confusing place for someone who is just trying to improve their way of life from either humdrum or unsocial to being able to take part in all the wondrous things they have read about or seen on TV or the internet. Searching for Self may help you to decide just what it is that you need to change in your life or perhaps you will find that you don't need to change anything at all, just look at life differently. Ancient Wisdom for the 21st Century may guide you through the maze of New Age ideas and ancient practices that are available. From the 1960s when we began to open our minds to many ideas that were hidden for a very long time, to the 21st century where we are able to search on-line for so many wondrous ideas, old and new. I hope this may help your journey.

SEARCHING FOR SELF

INTRODUCTION

I have been on this earth in this life for several decades now and during this current lifetime I have often taken different turns and had experiences that have either taught me new ideas or turned me off. Of the many lessons I have learned the most important one is to never stop looking. It may seem like a cliché, however we are only on this earth for a reasonably short time in our current form so why not make the most of it. I have studied different forms of healing, spirituality and healthy practices and I feel it is appropriate to share as much of this information as I can before heading off to the next life – whatever it might be. So please enjoy the read and remember, it is so much healthier to be positive and open to many things than it is to close down and never even look.

Many books, magazines and schools are expounding their beliefs and teachings to those who are seeking more than their fast moving world is providing for them. Finding the "right path" to follow is sometimes just a matter of meeting the right people, or maybe having the right kind of bank balance to cover the teachings of the modern guru. However, maybe it is just a matter of looking inside yourself to find what you have been looking for all over the place.

We are told constantly these days that we can do anything. Especially women. We can do anything we put our mind to – yeah right. At a price! Now that price can be physical, emotional or financial. But there is usually a price. Have you read the many articles on self improvement? Could it be that all self improvement needs is a good credit card so you can get along to the beauty salon, buy new clothes and take a course at $800 for a weekend of hype? But perhaps there is another way and that is to find out who you are *before* you try to improve yourself.

From the beginning of this life you have been taught and coached into being who you are now. Your conditioning began with the way you were born, the surroundings of your nursery, the clothes you were dressed in, the food you were given and the music your parents listened to. And all this before you even reached your first birthday. Then there were the restrictions placed on you once you began to walk, talk and act out your childhood fantasies. Unless you were lucky enough to belong to free spirited parents, all of a sudden you are placed in some form of organised group, whether it was kindergarten, childcare, playgroup or even a large family environment. Your conditioning still continued under the supervision of someone else. And so it was throughout your young life until all of a sudden after approximately 18 years you had to fend for yourself. You arrived at this point with all the wonderful, or otherwise, guidance of other people. Now who are you? You are most likely the product of someone else's guidance or teaching or you may have become a little twisted because your teachers were just a bit stranger than usual. With a bit of luck they were caring, loving individuals who had your welfare at heart and you came out OK in the end. There are many ways to describe someone who is 'normal' and if you take a real good look you will find that the so called normal people are in fact the odd ones out. If this sentence makes sense to you then consider yourself lucky as you have a very good slant on life.

Did you or did you not like the people who raised you?

Did they or do they live their lives the way you want to?

If you like who they are or were and you don't mind being a bit like them, with your personality thrown in, then what's the problem! The problem could be that someone has suggested that you could be better than you are. Are you happy with the way you are? Then leave well enough alone and enjoy the life you have made for yourself, making your own mistakes as you go along. However, you may find this book amusing anyway, so read on.

If you do have small improvements you would like to make to yourself, either physically, mentally or emotionally, then you just go ahead and do it. You don't need someone else's opinion or permission beforehand (unless it's illegal or affects someone else). Just do it. You can always undo it afterwards if you don't like it. However, if it is a major change you think might be required then please journey on.

SO WHO ARE YOU NOW?

Let's find out who you are. First of all you need to be on your own for a while so shut the world out or go and stay somewhere where you can be alone. Look at yourself in the mirror. Do you like what you see? I am not talking about your hairdo, or the pimple that just appeared on your nose this morning, or even the lovely wrinkles that have appeared over your many years, I am talking about you. The person inside. If you do like yourself then you are heading in the right direction. Skip the next two paragraphs. (No read them, you may be amused). If you don't like what you see then you need to find out why you don't. If it is a physical problem then we can leave that alone for a while because later on you may have changed your mind about your physical appearance and actually like yourself as you are. If it is the person you see behind the eyes then we are going to work on that anyway. The first thing we have to do is learn to like ourselves.

Take a <u>long</u> look at the person you see in the mirror. Somewhere along this life you *may* have begun to dislike yourself. Perhaps you did something to someone else that wasn't nice and you regretted this, or maybe someone began to tell you that you were not a nice person or you were useless, and you began to believe it. If someone tells you that you are bad or stupid often enough it is quite possible to begin to believe them. It doesn't necessarily mean it is true. However if you are bad or stupid then now is the chance to change that side of you. Please note that there are people who gain personal power by putting others down and you may have spent some time with one or more of these people. However it all started, we need to reverse the procedure and change things for the better.

You can <u>definitely</u> learn to love yourself once more, or at least gain the knowledge that you really are very nice. You probably liked yourself when you were very, very little. After all, whose toes were there, along with other parts of your anatomy, for you to play with? Yours – no one else's. So now, looking at yourself in the mirror, repeat the following affirmation;

"I AM A REALLY NICE PERSON"

or, if you have been mean or nasty to others you might light to say

"I AM REALLY SORRY I WAS MEAN AND WOULD LIKE TO ATONE FOR THIS"

or something similar.

This may feel a bit silly at first because we are discouraged from talking to ourselves, but once you get the hang of affirmations they really are quite easy. Besides, there is only you and the mirror so who is going to know. Now get on with it. You should repeat this over and over at least for a minute or two, take as long as you like. Then every day until you start to believe it, when you get up and are in the privacy of the bathroom look in the mirror and repeat it over and over again. *Every day please.* If you want to set yourself a goal of say 20 times a day then you will need something to help you count. Worry beads, Mala beads or prayer beads are handy. If you haven't used these before they are simply counting beads and usually have a gap or some other method of knowing when you get to the end. You hold them in your hand and each time you say your affirmation you move on to the next bead. So, if you have 25 beads on your string and you are going to repeat 50 times then you go around twice – get the idea? If you are one of the people reading this who are going to learn to love or at least like themselves again, then you are not to move on to the next paragraph until you have performed the above affirmation – once again "I AM A REALLY NICE PERSON".

Alright, you can now move on.

Eventually you will believe your affirmation, trust me, then you can continue to the next one; "I LOVE MYSELF WITH ALL MY HEART". Now this is a bit harder because you may have been taught that it is better to love others before oneself. But how do you know how to love someone else if you don't know what love is? Love is that warm feeling you get inside when something happens between you and another soul. It has nothing to do with sex. Sex can be one of life's little bonuses, right? Well self love is also a very warm feeling. If you were stuck on a desert island with nothing but the birds and fish for company, who would love you? You would, because you would eventually find out that you are your own best friend. (Although you might befriend a bird or fish to keep you company!)

OK maybe you can't get the self love bit right at this early stage, then at least try to think of yourself as your own best friend – because you are – and work on the love bit. That's a good start. So you can continue on.

Step one has been achieved or at least you are on the way, and it hasn't cost you any more than purchasing this book. It does seem very simple and that's because it really is. Don't try to make it difficult because it isn't. So now you have caught up with the people who already like themselves before they bought this book so we can carry on.

WHO ARE YOU – REALLY?

The most important lesson you can learn in order to change your life back to a self-loving, self-caring person that you were as a baby is to find out who you are. Who you were before becoming the adult you are today. The most important being in your life is you. So who are you? Past lives are not counted here, that is a different subject altogether. We are talking about the time from this birth to right now, this very moment.

Most of us cannot remember our birth, despite what some people tell you. It is possible to remember the early years though so that is the best place to start. Were you a little girl who loved pink and frills or a little boy who loved toy trucks? Or were you the other way round? Did you get lots of hugs and cuddles from your parents or guardians or were you left alone quite a lot? Was your life full of music and colour with a garden to play in or were you ignored while your parents sat around with other adults smoking and drinking and always talking adult stuff? Recognise yourself yet? If you were brought up in a happy household with outings, a place in the sun to play and good wholesome food and hugs and cuddles then that is very good, you had a good start. If you were one of the children who had to bring themselves up you may be strong and content also, that is what you need to think about. Were you a happy child? If the answer is no then you need to reclaim some of that childhood with music, nature, fun and company as you are nurtured by good healthy food and lifestyle. Eventually it will come through, then you have shaken off that feeling that you have missed out on something when you were very young. If you had a really bad time of it then I suggest that you need to talk to a professional Counsellor because there may be some very deep issues that need to be sorted out before you set out on your self improvement journey.

For now, let's proceed to the first step on your journey.

TIME OUT TO FIND YOUR INNER SELF

Inside your body is your real self. Now this may sound a bit odd but believe me, there is a "you" in there. Some people call it a soul, some call it the ego, some the spirit, but it is you and it is in there. Maybe you believe that when you die this "you" carries on in another body through reincarnation, maybe you believe you are transported off to heaven or hell or perhaps you believe that when the worms come all is gone. Whatever your belief for the hereafter, the present is what is concerning us at the moment and perhaps what you achieve now will help you in the hereafter anyway. What a bonus!

This "you" needs to be nourished and loved. It is very difficult to pay attention to yourself when everything around you is very busy, so time must be set aside on a regular basis to give yourself some attention. Ten minutes a day, thirty, or even more if you are retired or have some other reason for not filling up your day with work, children or school. In fact ten minutes every day is better than one hour once a week. This way your inner self gets the hang of being spoken to regularly. So please sort out your itinerary before going any further. If you are an early riser then you can spend some time before getting ready for the day or if you have a lunch hour and a quiet spot to escape to, then perhaps this would work for you.

How about the mums or dads who get up to a noisy family, send them off to school or wherever the rest of your household spends the day, then go to work themselves, come home, cook tea, do the washing, ironing and tomorrows lunches then fall into bed exhausted – then you will have to find ten minutes. How about shutting yourself in the bathroom for ten minutes somewhere around 10.30pm!! I know you will work it out because you always seem to be able to fit something extra in. This time *it's for you.* I remember being able to meditate whilst sitting in the car waiting for netball practice to finish. I would escape from home a little sooner than necessary just for that quiet time.

During the ten minutes you have set aside you need absolute peace. If you live in a noisy environment then try playing soft meditation music through earphones and light a nice smelling candle. Incense or an oil burner is a bonus. Mind you don't set the place on fire though. We don't want to spoil the peaceful time do we? So there you are sitting quietly on the floor, in a chair, on the bed (please don't lie down as you may fall asleep and that is not what you are trying to achieve), in the park, wherever you can, but please try to use the same place every time if you can. Make it your place, your shrine, your piece of space. Candles are nice to concentrate on because they have a calming effect on the mind, even an artificial one that flickers is better then none, or you can place a flower or beautiful picture of a scene from nature in front of you. Now, keeping your eyes open soften your gaze so that your eyes are out of focus and let your mind wander. First of all your thoughts will pop up like they are being released from an open can of worms. However, you must have a quick look at each thought then put it aside to be dealt with outside your private time. Right now we are going to try to clear your mind. Back to concentration on the candle, or the music, or the smoke drifting up from the incense, or whatever you have decided is the best for you. Begin to breathe deeply from the very bottom of your lungs. Try pushing your abdomen muscles out gently as you breath in to allow space for the lungs to expand and pull the muscles in when you breathe out. Breathe in through your nose filling the bottom of the lungs first and using your imagination fill the lungs to the top before holding for a few moments, then let it out through the nose (if you have a cold you can breath out through your mouth but only as a last resort) pushing the air up from the bottom of the lungs first until you push out the air at the top. By concentrating on your breathing you will begin to block out those other thoughts naturally. Only do the deep breathing for a few breaths then allow your breath to settle into a nice smooth flowing routine of normal breathing. Then it is just a matter of clearing your day to day thoughts and begin to concentrate on those thoughts that matter. The thoughts that pertain to your inner "self". The person inside you. The essence of your being. You are going to concentrate on love of your own self, love of the person you are, love of the body enclosing that self. This is acknowledging the "temple" that is your body and the "god or goddess" which is the self within. This is not religious and will not interfere with your religious beliefs, it is merely going within your own self. Eventually you will find this will help you with your religious or spiritual beliefs because what better way to be able to acknowledge the existence of a higher being that to be able to acknowledge the spirit within your own self? I have been teaching Yoga and Meditation for around 25 years at this stage and I can assure you that with practice you will develop your own meditation. Go to a class if you need to but not at the expense of any free time you now have. There have been only a very few people who have not been able to follow this simple form of meditation and I have encouraged them to just sit and listen to some peaceful music instead.

At this stage, this is all that is required. Please get this right before moving on to the next phase. You should practice this meditation throughout your life. It is not a thing that can just be done for a 10 week course then put aside. Make it a part of your life. If you can set up a little "shrine" with your incense, candles and something to play music then it will help you to get into the mood easier but this is not important. In fact a corner of the garden or on a verandah are excellent places to meditate and you won't need all the other bits and bobs. Watching a tree swaying in the breeze or a bee getting on with life is one of the best ways of taking your daily life stresses out of your mind. Gardening has long been known for it's therapeutic effects. So long as you can leave the rest of the world out of it and be by yourself. But in order to clear your mind it is not a good idea to be doing something that requires thought. So weeding is quite good for meditation so long as you don't accidentally pull out your new petunias!

As you begin to get the hang of spending some quiet time with yourself and find basic meditation is coming to you easily, then you may want to consider taking this a bit further.

BODY BEAUTIFUL - BODY HEALTHY

As you begin to feel better about the person you really are, it is time to look at the packaging. Is your body healthy? Is it overweight or underweight? Are there shadows under your eyes, ringing in your ears or your hair falling out? Can you walk up hills or stairs without passing out?

Depending on your answers, perhaps you need to tidy things up a bit, do some body "housekeeping", so where do you start? Start Easy. This will give you a chance to get used to the changes slowly (and you are less likely to give up)

First of all – Is your body healthy? The answer is a bit tricky because we all gauge "healthy" differently. So perhaps a quick medical checkup at either your GP or Naturopath is in order. Most health shops have convenient Iridology tests they do for a few dollars. Once you find out what has to be done then you know which direction you are headed.

Let's say you came out so healthy that you are dangerous to all those unhealthy people around you, then that is wonderful and you can maintain this healthy body by looking after it as it tumbles and stumbles through life. A healthy diet, plenty of sleep, relaxation and exercise is important even though you are very healthy, in order to stay that way. If you are young (under 40 – yes that's young) then you will probably get away with a bit of body abuse for a while, but guess what happens?? Down the track you will begin to creak a little and those late nights become a bit harder to catch up with by the time you get to 50 so look after that body please, it's the only one you've got. It really is amazing how much the body can take when it is young, but please don't get a false sense of security! Sooner or later you will begin to wonder how you kept up with yourself. However, there is hope yet and most of the damage can be undone with a little tender love and care of yourself. This is when you join in with the "unhealthy" people.

So you have had your checkup and now you know what you have to do in order to fix the little things that your lifestyle and genes have managed to stuff up. Let's say you just need to get fit. Your heart and lungs check out, your body eliminates when it ought to and you eat a healthy diet. You are the easy ones to sort out, all you need is motivation. That's the bit you have to work on. Motivation can mean just wanting to fit into a size smaller than you are now wearing (because you did last year) or it can be as simple as impressing the good looking man/woman you see every day at the bus stop. After all, who would be interested in a "loose muscled" although handsome/beautiful you? You'd be surprised how many people are interested in the real you not the exterior. Whatever your motive, you need to move – NOW – or the motivation will pass. If you haven't exercised for a while then you need to take it easy for a bit, warm up to it, don't go wearing yourself out on the first day. For starters you could take a walk. A nice stroll for about 10 – 15 minutes should do it. Look at the trees, smell the flowers, generally enjoy yourself. Don't be too slow though, you need to try and sweat a little. (Yes you are allowed to sweat, it's natural and is actually good for you. This eliminates nasty little toxins in your system.) Upon that subject, please look at your deodorant to make sure it doesn't contain aluminium. Don't ask me, Google it.

Now that all the non-healthy and the healthy-but-lazy people are out for a walk, you healthy-fit ones can go and do what it is that you do to keep so fit and come back to this book during your relaxation time.

There, that wasn't so hard was it? You have walked about 15 minutes, hopefully a few times during the week, and you are feeling a bit looser. So we come to jogging. I have never had much time for it myself, it seems that I can get just as fit walking briskly so I do. When you are well built in the female department then jogging is not much fun. Your upper body gets more exercise than the rest of you and seeing yourself jog past a shop window is enough for you to reach out for the number of the nearest breast reduction clinic (which is counter productive to the self love department so don't even think of it). However, if your medical person gives you the OK to jog and you really want to then off you go. Now there are many ways to exercise and you must decide which is best for you. Many years ago I had a job which required me to spend lots of hours in my car, staying in motels and eating "on the road" food. So I had to find some way of exercising whilst in this situation. I took myself off to Qigong lessons and began a regime that I still practice several times each week 30 years later. This, combined with my gardening, keeps me healthy, although I would never be able to run a long way and never could. I can, however, walk the socks off those supposedly fitter than me when it comes to getting around the markets and you should see me move if I have a bus or train to catch. My mother was a strider not a walker and had reasonably long legs so childhood was always brisk and it stuck. So when it comes down to being healthy it is only a matter of point of view.

If you would like to combine what you have learned so far, liking yourself, getting healthy and fit then please try Yoga, Pilates, Tai Chi or Qigong along with your gym, walking, running or other strenuous exercise. They are all gentle forms of exercise and most incorporate meditation within their practice. There are also a few different forms of Yoga from the very simple to the extreme. Hatha Yoga, which is the form that I teach, is the most common and you can find a teacher through the Yellow Pages, local newspaper or perhaps your local health shop has a Notice Board with names on it. Power Yoga is becoming popular for those who might think Yoga is for sissies and there's Hot Yoga that is definitely not for red headed, Scottish/English people like me who head for the shade when the heat reaches 26c. Even though I live in Central Queensland. However, you will find that if you have spent half your life in a gym pumping iron that you may be surprised at the workout you will get at a normal yoga class. If you are already fit and want to incorporate exercise and spirituality and like to move about a bit, why not try some of the forms of martial arts that incorporate meditation. There are a few around these days and can usually be found at the local Youth centres. For those of us who are happy moving slowly then Tai Chi or Qigong is definitely the way to go, good exercise, healthy breathing and you won't go red in the face and fall over covered in sweat when you are finished!

SO YOU THINK YOU'RE GETTING OLD

What's this got to do with New Age thinking you may be asking? Well it has a lot to do with it. Once upon a time we were retired off by the age of 65 and were considered to be old. Not mature but **Old.** This thinking ended up with a lot of folk who are full of knowledge and great ideas being palmed off to retirement homes or forgotten by the rest of society. Once or twice a year we were given outings such as Mothers Day and Fathers Day but generally we were considered too old to join in many things. Thankfully this attitude has changed and now it is not uncommon to find someone in their 70s going to University or learning new skills. Where the New Age comes into it is that either we "oldies" are teaching many of these subjects to the young or we are being encouraged to go along and learn them ourselves. My own journey began well back in my 30s but to this day, a few decades later, I am still finding fantastic new ideas to keep me healthy and strong in body and mind and my spiritual journey is amazing. I am very pleased that within the so-called New Age community my opinion is often called for regarding the knowledge I have gained over those decades. Once upon a time elders were revered for their knowledge and wisdom and I do not want reverence. However, with so called modern society this elder knowledge is not always appreciated outside traditional societies and nationalities and as a result the wisdom of old age is not considered important any more. But this is changing.

Old age is a state of mind they say. However, if you are getting on a bit and you creak when you get up and there are more grey hairs these days than coloured ones, then you might be interested in this. *Old age is not a state of mind, but feeling old is.* As we progress through our current life there will be lots of young people telling you that you only *think* you're old and lots more trying to convince you that you are 'past it' 'Over the hill' or any other cliché they can think of to make you feel like you are dried up and ancient. However, I am going to try to convince them and you that they are wrong.

First of all, when you get up in the morning and you creak a bit, it could be that you don't move around enough, or perhaps you are on the wrong diet and don't include enough of the good things that lubricate your joints. So you could begin with your diet. Off you go to the local health shop and have a *free* chat with the resident naturopath, most health shops have them these days. Tell them you need advice, you don't have hoards of money to spend and are more interested in finding out what can help you all over instead of one piece of you at a time. Adding certain oils to your diet helps the creaks and groans, the naturopath will let you know which is the best for you. There are many wonderful books around to help you sort out your diet. Perhaps you might be one of the lucky ones with a GP who thinks holistically instead of giving you painkillers and anti this and that.

Quite a few people think that as they get older, especially if they live by themselves, that they don't need to cook properly or worry so much about fresh fruit and vegetables in their daily diet. They may also think that protein and calcium are things young people need to build healthy bodies with. Well, guess what? Except for your central nervous system and your brain, your body is continually renewing itself, in fact there is a seven-year turnaround from the time most pieces of you renews itself. So if you change bad habits and begin to do the right thing by, say your liver, then your liver has a good chance of renewing itself after seven years so long as your other bits don't break down too much and put a lot of strain on this renewing liver. What this means is that should you decide that you want to get fit, healthy and live long and prosper (sorry, can't help myself I'm an old Trekkie) then you have to look after the whole body and soul not just use a band-aid approach to parts of you that aren't doing so well. In order to prove this theory, think of this. Most of us are born with fully working parts. The body is programmed from conception to work properly, unless you are one of the unlucky ones to have inherited problems from your parents. Lets just say you are one of the lucky ones who had all your parts in good order from the womb. As you go through life your body is ageing at the same speed all over. Your legs are as old as your head and your heart is as old as your big toe. Got the idea? So how come that when you get a stiff or sore shoulder and you are over 60 you blame it on old age? How could your shoulder be old and not your belly button when they are the same age? So what causes the sore shoulder? Not old age but a problem with your shoulder. Now this could stem from your spine being out of alignment or you may have knocked it on something or you might be trying to lift a weight in an awkward manner. Whatever the cause of the sore shoulder it is not old age! If you have arthritis in your hands it is not from old age but from some other problem you have developed over the years – otherwise everyone would have arthritis and they don't. So if you are creaking and groaning then don't blame it on old age, go and see a chiropractor or osteopath and they will tell you if it's your skeleton or if you can't afford it then go see your GP, but please, don't let them just give you pain killers because you are a senior citizen, ask for the problem to be investigated and get it fixed. All the painkillers will do is take away the pain, they will not fix the problem. The same goes for arthritis. There are some good natural ways of helping arthritis and they do work and something in your diet may be causing that imbalance. If your GP just wants to give you drugs please go and chat with a naturopath (at the same friendly health shop) to find out what you can use. In the meantime we are going for a walk!

Exercise is as important as diet in slowing up the "ageing" process. I am not suggesting you join a gym or take up soccer. However, I am suggesting that you take a walk. This is the best form of exercise you can give your body. While you are walking, swinging your arms, striding out, you are exercising all your limbs. If you look around you at the same time then you are exercising your neck muscles. So off you go. If you haven't been out for a while then you will discover new things. There are trees and shrubs to look at, neighbourhood gardens, even the neighbours themselves. Please don't use the excuse that you live in a boring neighbourhood because if you haven't been walking around it lately the trees and other plants will look different now to the way they looked last time you went out and there might even be new neighbours. Now what's your next excuse? Raining? Then wear a raincoat!

As I live in the country we find it a health hazard to try to go walking at night or even at dusk because there are no street lights and you can get severely run over walking on the road (no footpaths you see), so a friend of mine has developed herself a walking track around the perimeter of her 5 acre property. Her dog happily goes with her and she does this route a few times each day. Just to keep her company the neighbour's horse does the length of their adjoining fence with her. This way, the lovely neighbour gets her exercise and so do her dog and the horse. Amazing how one person exercising can motivate others isn't it?

A few years ago I spent 6 weeks wearing a plaster boot following an accident and I must say that anyone on crutches is definitely excused from all other forms of exercise during that period where they are delegated onto one foot and two crutches. I had more exercise during that 6 weeks than usual. There is more than ability involved to be able to heave oneself up and propel oneself around in that ungainly manner and the doctor made sure I didn't put any weight at all on that foot by making the sole of it pointed towards the floor. If I tried to stand on it I fell over. Simple method of control by the doctor. My biceps and left leg had definitely grown during that time and during the first week I could feel my heart beating faster in 5 minutes than after a 30 minute brisk walk. Perhaps we should develop an aerobic exercise program to be done while one leg is tied up to render it useless while you balance on crutches. We could even have "designer crutches" – no, let's not go down that track.

GARDENING AS THERAPY AND/OR MEDITATION

During the Covid pandemic and lockdowns many people took to gardening for the first time in their lives. From pots on a balcony to a full blown backyard farm and every other way folk could think of to plant and grow something gardens big and small were created. One of the great benefits of this was healthier eating and exercise, however there was also the greater benefit of creating calmness. It is logical that fruit and vegetables that have been picked and eaten within the same day are going to be healthier than produce that has spent days, weeks and even months travelling from the place it was grown to your table. Eggs from your own chickens or those of a neighbour where the chickens are able to roam around finding worms and other goodies are so much better for you (and the chicken) than from some huge shed where they are kept out of sunlight for their entire laying lives. I have been quite lucky over the past 12 years when I found that apart from having my own chickens I can also buy free range eggs from either our local weekly market or the butcher in town.

The exercise factor of gardening is a no-brainer. Dig, bend, lift, stretch and so many other benefits and, unlike the local Gym, it's free. I call my garden My Gym and try to spend 1.5 to 2 hours most mornings out there getting my workout. The mental and emotional benefits are huge because when it's just you with your spade or trimmer its all about the Mindfulness that some people spend lots of money learning about. It just happens.

So where and when could you start to create your own garden if you haven't already done so? Start at your local garden centre, read books, watch a garden show on TV, join a garden club or grab a spade and fork, a pot plant or whatever is on hand, but start. If you already have one on the go then out you go, stop reading for an hour or so and see what you need to do with what you already have. One great starter is to buy a reasonable size pot with herbs growing in it already and just put it outside your kitchen. Make sure it's not in the full mid-day sun and remember to water it every few days and there you have your first "garden". Picking fresh herbs for something you are cooking is an amazing start to what may become a passion, or if you are a very busy person you will have a ready supply of something as simple as parsley at your doorstep.

If you have a potato, or more than one, sprouting in the vegetable section of your cupboard find a fair size plant pot put about 20cm of potting mix or soil in the bottom, lay your sprouting potato, or potatoes, sprouting side up on the dirt and cover it with about the same amount of soil. Give it a drink about once a week then when the sprouts grow up through the soil wait till the leafy bits are about 20cm and cover again with soil leaving the top green leafy bits above the surface. Keep doing that till the pot is full then leave it. When the top dies off in about 2-3 months time then push your hand down into the dirt and you should have potatoes. Lovely little ones that taste delicious steamed then buttered with some chopped up parsley. If you leave them a little longer you will have bigger ones. There you go, you have grown your first crop of potatoes. Yes it is that easy. Don't let the soil get dry or too wet and make sure it gets sunlight for at least half the day. If you haven't got a big enough pot then you can use a big plastic bag – or one of the ones that are made for that purpose from your garden centre. One note here for the country readers. Farmers and responsible gardeners who are growing potatoes out in the garden will usually use Certified Seed Potatoes because it is easy for disease to spread in a crop. This is not a problem if you are growing in a couple of pots or in an enclosed garden where the soil will not be leaving the garden on someone's shoes so go ahead and use the sprouting ones you left too long in the cupboard if you are not out in the country and planting in the open.

Planting food plants that are in season will give you a much better start than trying to grow something complicated. If you don't want to grow food plants then start with succulents because they very rarely die on you. In the garden or in pots begin with natives if you can so ask the local garden centre what grows well in your area – stress of decision gone. In Central Queensland we can plant tomatoes, eggplants, beans and all kinds of squash things that are required for a Mediterranean diet throughout Autumn, Winter and Spring. Growing such things that won't grow down south in winter will usually flourish up here but the usual summer stuff usually goes to seed with too much humidity in Summer. Over the years I have experimented with other plants and some have grown but others failed. Note for the Queenslanders – don't even try to grow Brussel Sprouts north of Maryborough – they pop open around about August and they aren't supposed to do that. Usually I stick with what grows best. However whatever I am growing the act of planting, nurturing and then eating is very satisfying when I have picked it from my own garden. Then there are flowers. What grows best in your area? Look around at other people's gardens and see what flourishes and check out your local Council gardens. The peaceful nature of gardening goes out the window if you are continually stressing over some plant that wasn't meant to grow in your area. And you need flowers if you want to grow most vegetables because you need bees for pollination. Unless, like many of us, you have that little paint brush to hand pollinate pumpkin. For those who might be allergic to *bee stings* consider encouraging Native Stingless Bees into your garden. There may be someone in the area who can show you how to get your own hive then you have your own personal pollinators. However, you will have to make sure you have native flowering plants or they will leave home and find somewhere that has. Make sure you are not using any pesticides in your garden though, you will kill any kind of bee that comes in contact with them. There are many ways to control pests that don't require spraying.

Now, while you are out there gardening start thinking of the herbs and medicinal plants (no not that one – it's illegal in Australia). Many herbs have medicinal value but please remember to get sound advice from a naturopath or other educated source. I have found that there are quite a few GP's who are quite happy to give good advice on this subject but if yours says it's all rubbish then either change your doctor or go and ask someone who knows, like your local Health Food shop. Meanwhile there are some easy ones that have been around for millennia such as Mint, Chamomile, Rosemary, Parsley and Sage. Yes there is a song there. Mint is good for the digestion and is very good at keeping mice out of the house. By the way, don't plant mint directly into the garden as it will probably go rampant and you will wish you hadn't done that. Keep it in pots. Rosemary is very good for the memory, that's why it's a symbol for Anzac Day. A cup of Rosemary tea each day is good when you are studying, or put a couple of drops of Rosemary oil in your oil burner. Sage has a similar effect on the brain but I have used Sage as a throat gargle or for a chesty cough most of my life (thanks mum) and my adult children still use it too. Parsley helps your iron levels and as we use it frequently as a garnish then many people are getting the benefits without even knowing about it. Chamomile is well known to aid sleep and as a calmative or it's just nice for a cup of afternoon tea.

There are many plants that are used as medicine or just to keep us healthy. The best thing to do is buy a good book on the subject and ***remember, they are medicine so make sure what you choose does not contradict any medication you may be on***. The best person to ask about this is a professional. One example is that if you are on some heart medications you should not use licorice in any form except maybe the sweets because they very rarely contain any actual Licorice. So get sound advice if you are already taking medicine.

Interesting Fact: Celery was medicinal long before it landed in the kitchen. Hippocrates (That clever Greek) recommended it's use and it appears in Chinese medicine around the 5th Century CE. Practitioners of Ayurveda use it for a variety of problems.

Back in time it was a wild plant and was quite different from the cultivated version we have today. But it is still very good for you. I keep a pot on the verandah with one Celery plant in it and just snip off what I need for cooking. It doesn't grow into that great big succulent plant that it will in the garden. If you grow it in the garden it will keep on giving for a couple of years so don't pull the plant out when you need celery for your salad.

If you are a busy person who doesn't have much time to go poking around in the garden when you are about to make dinner then do what I have done and keep several pots near the back door with your favourite herbs in. Then, at the moment of creation, you can just go out and pick what you need instead of buying a whole bunch and wasting half of it. Parsley, mint, thyme, chives and many other herbs love being in a pot. Just make sure the pot is big enough and gets plenty of light. Mine don't even get the sun in the winter but they are in the light and that seems to be all they need. Herbs used in cooking will have most of the benefits you need unless you have been told by a naturopath that you need concentrated quantities. So grow them, use them and enjoy the health benefits while spending a little time each week looking after them.

So happy gardening everyone, it can become quite therapeutic in a very short time.

YOU – THE NICE PERSON

Do you think that you are a nice person? Even if you *have been* the meanest person on the block, you have been nice to one person by reading this book and that is YOU. That's a pretty good start you know. You have set aside some time to spend with yourself. Not bad company are you? Or if you think you could be better it is up to you to change, not for someone else to do it for you. If other people think you aren't nice then perhaps you need to stay away from those people or see what you can do to change that part of you. However if you can stay away from those people anyway why not leave the worry of being nice out of it and get on with life. So you are a bit of a hermit, like your own company. Fine, that was what you may have set out to achieve. So you are a success already. Do you like the feeling?

You will find as time goes by, that in liking your own company you will be more pleasant for others to be around you. Set the rules. You like to be by yourself at times and others should respect that. If they don't then they have the problem not you. See, you are a nice person; you like to be with you. We did it didn't we? What a nice couple of people we are!

By now you may have discovered that life is not just about how much money you have or have not, or what material possessions you own. In fact you should be just about ready to turn a corner. You may be ready to discover that there is more to discover about this "New Age" thing that everyone has been talking about and ready to throw yourself into it headlong and learn all you can. Wrong. You need to learn about this amazing phenomena one step at a time.

Have you ever wanted to do something that you have not been able to achieve for one reason or another? I am not talking about those things that cost lots of money and time, but perhaps you would like to learn to sing, play music, do Tai Chi, grow flowers, act on stage. Anything that requires more of an effort than money. Well now that you have learnt to like/love yourself then you are ready to do something for yourself. Music can be learned at many different levels. If you have no ear for music at all then just enjoy listening to others play. Go to free or cheap concerts, local musical gigs, school concerts, anything that doesn't require loads of money and time to get there. If you have a bit of an ear for music then pick up something and play. Even a tin whistle or a mouth organ. If you are really good at keeping time drumming your fingers on something while the music plays, try doing that on a small drum. You can actually do your good deed here and buy yourself one of those little drums from the Community Aid Abroad shops and help a third world country at the same time. Take the little drum home and next thing you know you are keeping time on your little drum instead of a table top! Drumming is a very good "New Age" thing. Not only is it fun but it is actually very good for the spirit within as well. If you want to add a bit more noise then buy a tambourine - but I have been told many years ago by the other members of the band I sang with that not everyone likes the sound of that one (they took it off me and taught me the guitar) so check first with the people you live with. Don't bother about being the best, just enjoy it for yourself. Go out in the yard and sing while you garden. (No you can't meditate while you are doing two other things). Dance while you do the housework. No one will see those hips swing to the beat of a calypso rhythm, and men can enjoy this too, or watch you sweep across the room as your mobile phone plays a Tango (yes, mine did, I found it in the menu while I was setting something else up but now it greets me with a Hindi chant). Learn the guitar. Find a friend to teach you for a meal you cook for them. Tai Chi or Yoga can be followed just about anywhere for a few dollars a week or for Seniors there are some free Tai Chi classes run by a local Council. (Or again find a friend etc.....), and once you learn the basics you can practice on your own either in the house or the garden. Flowers or veggies can be grown for the cost of a packet of seed or save your own from previously grown plants. But please be nice to your bees and don't spray your garden with nasty chemicals. I know I have already said that but it is very important. Acting is just a matter of joining a local theatrical group. They are all amateurs so don't worry about your prowess on stage. Besides, they will probably welcome a newcomer with open arms.

So now you have moved on and begun another of those "New Age" things, you have begun to learn something for yourself.

How do you feel? You may have discovered the person inside you. The one who has always wanted to play three blind mice on the tin whistle, the one who always wanted to grow their own tomatoes, the one who knew they could recite Shakespeare if only they had the opportunity, or the one who enjoyed the tranquillity of quiet time spent in their own mind.

Moving on from this lesson is just a matter of progression. If you enjoy a little tune on the whistle but would like to take it further, then perhaps you might like to graduate to a flute or recorder (very cheap to buy). Want to dance the Tango a little better or take up Belly Dancing? Look for a teacher on line, through your local newspaper or put an ad in yourself to find one. If you have enjoyed planting and growing flowers, then go a bit further. Plant a veggie garden in the back yard or on your patio in pots, and by using natural fertiliser and garlic sprays you will provide your table with healthy fresh food. It is as easy as following hints in books or on TV shows written by people who know what they are talking about. Or ask a friend. Should you find you like to act then look for lessons through your local learning facility or neighbourhood centre and meet others with similar interests. The same goes for Tai Chi or Yoga. You will find that the more you do it the more you will want to and it will become part of your life. If you are lucky enough to have a little bit of land to play with you could graduate to a little bit of mini farming. Chickens are a delight to look after and if you have children they will get in on this one. I have found chickens to be the best companions outside of the immediate best friend category. They will happily follow you around, sit beside you, make delightful little noises and come to you any time you want to proffer food. On top of that they will happily give you lovely fresh eggs and clean up your veggie scraps. Oh yes, they are also very good at getting the bugs out of your vegetables. All you have to do for them is provide a very safe place to spend the night and feed and water them. Plus a few other little comforts. There is plenty of literature on the subject and anyone who has kept a few for a considerable time will happily tell you all about what needs to be done. Ducks are nice too if you have a dam for them to swim on. But I digress, that's another story.

Now so far we have concentrated on doing things that YOU want to do, not your family, not your workmates, not your nosy neighbour, but YOU. And by doing these wonderful things for yourself you will find that you enjoy doing things for others more than you did before. Another of life's bonuses! Makes you feel good doesn't it? So what's this got to do with New Age you ask? Well, there are many wonderful things involved in this New Age idea that are there to heal your body, mind and spirit and that's about you. Other people are responsible for themselves and although its alright to help them on their way it's only possible for change to happen to someone if they really want it to. There are many who spend their lives helping others only to find that at the end of the day they have neglected themselves. There is an old saying "You can't help someone else properly if you don't help yourself."

ANCIENT WISDOM FOR THE 21ST CENTURY

ENTERING THE "NEW AGE"

Having been a teenager in the 60s and a young adult and mother by the mid 70s I was right in the middle of the Age of Aquarius and the hippie movement. While I was hanging out with Surfies in my bikini in the 60s listening to the surfing sounds, such as Bombora and Wipeout I remember friends taking off to join the new community out at Nimbin and by the mid 70s many were off to buy a piece of land in the country and set themselves up to be self sufficient. I saw the mini skirt arrive and then the clothing that arrived from India in wonderful bright colours. We learned tie dying, macrame and many other interesting and colourful activities. People were discovering that their bodies didn't have to be hidden and women were beginning to find that they were just as capable as men to do things that had been denied them in the past. Out of this change came natural therapies, crystal and oil healing, herbalism, energy healing, Reiki and many other natural healing modalities that had been around for thousands of years but suppressed by religion and societies. The re-emergence of Paganism and Wicca gained momentum and it became OK to be gay. It took a few more decades but thankfully today most people will accept that someone who treats illness with oils, herbs and other ancient methods is not a quack or witch. My mother used herbal teas for healing when I was a child and rubbed a mixture of eucalyptus oil and something to carry it on our chests when we had a cold – and that was in the 1950s.

Whether you are a teenager, young adult, parent, middle aged working suburbanite, tree changer or elderly it matters not. If you want to learn about all the things I have taken for granted in my life and can share with you then read on my friend. I shall attempt to demystify some it for you or at least stir up your curiosity to learn more. Let's continue this journey.

THE JOURNEY

Since the early 20th century many people have researched and experimented with ancient methods of healing, divination and lifestyle choices. The search continues to this day. However during the 1960s life changed in so many ways for many people and we began to be given the opportunity to learn so much more when barriers were taken down allowing many people to learn about how things were done before science took over. Natural Therapy colleges opened throughout the modern world and although some of this information was withheld by religion, and sadly some is still taboo today, we were able to access so much if that is what we required.

Natural therapies, as they are known today, were normal healing therapies before modern medicine and science took the lead. Modern medicine became the leader as science developed new and complicated treatments where the patient was usually kept in the dark by the practitioner and given the medicine or treatment that was recommended. However, there were also many folk who began to research the ancient methods and the herbs that their grandmother might have used to great effect. From this search for something different and natural came a resurgence in alternative collages of healing where a person who wished to become a healer using natural methods could go along and spend 5 years or more learning such things as herbalism, massage therapy, aromatherapy, homeopathy and interesting modalities like crystal therapy, colour and sound therapy and others. So we are going to take a look at some of these modalities that are now very much mainstream in the 21st century along with a look at such 'New Age' interests that have been around since before history was written down by the Romans.

I would like to say here that if you are looking into using natural therapies and treatment to deal with a serious illness then please let your physician or specialist know what you are doing and be very aware that natural medicine, herbal, vitamins or other treatments may not go along with any mainstream medicine or treatment that you are taking. Always consult a qualified natural therapist and not just someone who has read all the books and done a weekend course.

NATURAL THERAPIES

AND OTHER HEALING MODALITIES

Throughout my life I have tried to use natural therapies to keep my body healthy and have taken advice on such things as using Aromatherapy, Ayurveda, Massage therapy, Homeopathy, Crystals and other modalities. I try to avoid taking any kind of drugs, although if I had a serious illness I would certainly take the advice of my doctor as well as my natural therapist. I am not going to give you health advice on these subjects because apart from two of these I have no training in the others. First of all my advice is to make sure the person who is giving the advice is a professional with the training to do so. As with many things in this life there are charlatans and do-gooders who may give you advice, in good faith, that is not backed up by training and expertise. However, most Health Food shops in Australia have trained Naturopaths on hand who can guide you along if you can't afford a consultation. If you are in a Health Fund or Health Insurance then most cover some natural therapies and not others. Within your community there may be natural therapists practising and there may also be someone with very good knowledge of how to stay healthy, physically and mentally, who can guide you on your way. A properly trained fitness instructor may also be well versed in diet as well as exercise and many fitness centres also have a dietitian on staff. A practitioner of Traditional Chinese Medicine usually also offers acupuncture and there are many massage therapists out there who have been trained in other natural therapies. One practitioner I know combines the use of Yoga with her natural therapies treatments so the patient is able to use the physical and meditation aspects of these modalities along with the treatment given in the clinic. Many natural therapies combine more than one modality, Ayurveda is a good example, so the whole body is 'treated' not just the one complaint. So as you read the following pages please keep a very open mind if you are new to this way of healing and healthy living.

AYURVEDA

This is science of looking after the whole body and mind that has it's origins in India and is believed to be the oldest surviving healing system with trained practitioners, apart from natural healing practised by traditional inhabitants in countries such as Australia. Ayurveda is still practised today in many countries of the world and it's practitioners are kept up to date with the modern take on the whole system. The whole body and mind are treated, not just the symptoms, as happens in many modern treatments. The treatment will look at not only your diet but your general lifestyle, spiritual awareness, psychology and many other factors. Some practitioners will also include Astronomy and/or Astrology in their treatments.

According to Ayurveda everyone has a combination of the three Doshas or 'biological humours' that rule our constitution, Vata, Pita and Kapha, that are centred around the 5 elements. These Doshas regulate the body and mind and in order to find out what your Dosha type is you will be questioned about your lifestyle, the date of your birth and many other questions that would not normally come into the conversation with your GP. However, some Ayurvedic practitioners will concentrate on diet and exercise and will advise you on eliminating or adding certain foods in order to make the body sort itself out over time. There are not many qualified practitioners in Australia at this time sadly, however this is changing as the interest in alternative forms of healing become more popular and new practitioners are trained. There is a lot of use of such herbs and spices that you find in Asian cooking such as turmeric and you may already have a good supply in your pantry or can purchase them at an Asian supermarket or on line. If you can't find a practitioner in your area then ask around as it is possible that there is a practitioner near enough for you to go for a session who doesn't advertise. Once again, ask at your local health store as they will most likely be able to help you. Many Naturopaths have also trained in Ayurveda so again, ask around or search the internet for your local area.

AROMATHERAPY

Essential oils can be used to enhance the mind, mood and/or emotions. They have been used in one form or another for thousands of years and have been a "tool" for healers or just used by everyday folk during that time. In our modern times many of these oils are used in modern medicine, cosmetics, food and cleaning products and many of the common oils have been cloned or copied to give the aroma or taste of the real oil. There are so many uses for countless oils and I am not going to go into details for different oils, for that you need to consult one of the many books on the subject or once again, speak to a practitioner. However, *I will begin with a caution*. They should be used with care and before using any of them you need to know that they are concentrated and require a very small amount – so check the directions on the bottle first. Dumping a whole bottle of certain oils into an oil burner or into your bath could end up making you quite ill. Usually only 2 to 3 drops in a saucer of water on the oil burner is sufficient. The same goes for a bath. Pouring a bottle of lavender oil into your bath will probably make you feel unwell and could just put you to sleep. I had a client once who did just that and ended up in hospital because she passed out in the bath after ignoring my advice. So, caution please. Using the oil burner in your room with the correct amount of oil and water can enhance your mood, calm you down or just make the place smell nice. These days we can buy an oil burner that runs on power and puts out just the right amount of aroma. Another caution is that some oils will burn your skin if applied neat. Be careful. If you are advised by someone to use an oil neat on your skin to heal something then please remember to try a very small amount first.

However, there are a couple of oils that I find invaluable around the house. Tea Tree Oil – applied to the collar of your shirt or on the ends of sleeves (just a little) or mixed with water and sprayed on your arms usually keeps flies and mosquitoes away and it is also a good one to use as a disinfectant. You can actually buy premixed Tea Tree oil for that purpose. Eucalyptus oil is also an excellent disinfectant, we use it for cuts etc and I have been using it to disinfect my Covid face masks because I refuse to buy throw away ones, just a drop or two of Eucalyptus or Tea Tree oil in a small amount of warm water washes it just fine. However its a good idea to rinse it out because the smell can be a bit too much when you put the mask on. Just make sure you are placing no more than a couple of drops in about 150ml of warm water. Then my other favourite is Peppermint oil. Mice and ants do not like it at all. I like to smear it neat on a windowsill where the ants have found a way in and they don't bother coming back. For mice I've found that mixing the Peppermint oil in water – about 1-100ml and spray where you think mice might be coming in will deter them. Keeping a plant pot near the door with mint growing in it also has a deterrent effect and it is nice and handy if you want to use it in the kitchen. We had a problem with a mouse making itself comfortable in the base of a lounge chair, it had chewed away the lining underneath and found it a very cosy place to be. We sprayed the place with Peppermint oil after catching said mouse and removing it outside (we don't kill things) to make sure it didn't find it's way back there – and it didn't. Just a note on that point. If you remove such a beastie from your premises then make sure you take it about 200 metres at least from your home before letting it go as they *will* find their way back.

So there are many ways you can use essential oils but please remember, they can be quite powerful so use as directed. And my last note on that, Essential Oils are different from those nice smelling oils you can buy to just make the house smell nice. Make sure you are getting Essential Oils if you want to use them for healing, cleaning or cooking. It will say it on the label.

FLOWER REMEDIES

AUSTRALIAN BUSH FLOWER

AND BACH REMEDIES

Over the past few decades we have been introduced to Australian Bush Flower remedies. The flowers are collected, mostly in the wild, then once they have been turned into essences they are used for many reasons. Most of the time they are combined with Aromatherapy treatment or other natural healing but they can also be incorporated into essential oils for such as massage, sprayed into a room to enhance learning or study and decrease stress. They are perfectly safe to use. There is also the equivalent in other countries, such as South America and Europe and have been used for a very long time. There is an excellent range of books and information available and I have found the work of Ian White to be invaluable. You can do a course that allows you to gather and prepare your own range of essences so if you would like to look further into this please do so. They are available ready made in many health food shops and one that I have used is the Emergency Essence Mist. You may also know of the Bach Flower remedies and these are similar.

HOMEOPATHY

Homeopathy is a holistic form of healing, in other words the whole body and mind are treated not just the symptoms that are obvious. To simplify how it works your body's defence system is built up to fight whatever is causing your imbalance. Usually the practitioner will use other methods of healing alongside any "medicine" you are given. You will also be asked about your diet, exercise, environment and stresses so that the practitioner can work out the best treatment for you. The principal of "Like can cure like" is an important component so an illness can be cured or assisted by giving you a treatment that has similar symptoms to the ones you have. The Greek physician Hippocrates in the 5th century BC expounded this theory because he didn't believe the common misconception that illness was divine intervention and that the body was capable to healing itself with the right treatment. The Romans also used a form of Homeopathy and about 300 years ago it was given it's present title by Samuel Christian Hahneman in Germany. Albert Schweitzer (1875-1965) expressed Homeopathy in the following words *"Within every patient there resides a doctor and we as physicians are at our best when we put our patients in touch with the doctor inside themselves."*

CHAKRAS

You may have heard people talking about Chakras and thought to yourself that it sounded a bit far fetched that something like different colours and concentration upon different parts of your body was just a bit "out there" for you. If you have attended a Yoga class you may have heard your teacher talk of such things and in fact there might be a chart on the wall of your naturopath or health food shop showing strange signs. It's all a bit mysterious isn't it? Well it is not and many energy healing modalities use these Chakras in their practice.

Throughout the body there are 7 major and many minor energy circles where the body stores energy then distributes this through your nervous, endocrine and blood systems. If these Chakras become blocked, then your body reacts eventually by virtue of problems with your health, either physical or mental. In order to clear the blockage certain meditation or some other healing modality such as massage on one or all of these Chakras is performed. There are simple ways you can do this to yourself without the need for another person. However there is much more involved in the practice of Chakra clearing so until you learn a method that suits you then you should be guided by someone who knows the best way to do it. Chakra meditation is practised in some instances by visualising a colour which corresponds with each Chakra or various crystals that correspond with a particular Chakra may be placed on the body. It's not quite that simple of course, but that is the general idea. If you would like to take this further please contact someone with expertise in Chakra balancing or perhaps a yoga teacher, Reiki healer or other person who practises this wonderful method of healing. Once you learn how to do it then Chakra meditation regularly assists your body to be more stable and will react to life in a more positive way. If all this sounds a bit far fetched, many medical experts throughout the world use Chakra balancing in their healing and even some medical scientists have admitted that there is "something there".

MEDITATION AND SPIRITUALITY

I have discussed using meditation to relax and rid yourself of the stresses of every day life in a previous chapter and how it can be used to heal yourself mentally and physically. However, many different meditations can be practised to guide you towards a spiritual path. This can be an extension of the Chakra meditation, or can be solely for the purpose of finding your way spiritually. If you have found yourself without any spiritual beliefs for one reason or another, then perhaps you might like to feel your way around some of the "new age" ideas. Spirituality does not necessarily mean taking up a religion. Religion usually means following an organisation or ideal that has a set of rules or tenets put down at some stage by humans with or without divine assistance. However, this is not the only way to reach a higher

Being, Spirit or God. You can do it yourself through meditation and education.

Reaching the spirit world is a subject that can be discussed forever. Depending on how far you want to go, there is no end to the time and effort you can spend on the subject. It is a wonderful feeling when you reach the stage where you can quietly connect to a higher Being through either thought or the spoken word. To be able to just talk to that Being about your day, ask for guidance or plead for help. Whatever you need, there is nothing more required to connect than to sit quietly and turn within yourself as suggested earlier for basic meditation then attune to the object of your attentions and get on with it. No one is going to listen to you except the higher being you are connected to. No earthly being need know what it is you are discussing. This is between you and your higher being. Nice and easy isn't it? Well it should be. For centuries man and his gods have discussed and solved problems, taken care of business and generally had the kind of relationship that can never be found with another living human being. Worth thinking about isn't it? Don't need a higher being telling you what to do? Easy. When you connect to your inner self it is very possible to find answers to questions you may have by simply blocking out the rest of the world and actually listening to what you have to say to yourself. In order to act on whatever you find then it comes down to your own ethics and morals to make decisions.

YOGA, QIGONG AND TAI CHI

YOGA

Having been a teacher of Yoga and Qigong for over 24 years I would like to share a little of what I know. In our society and in other Western cultures Yoga is practiced as a form of physical exercise that can be combined with a spiritual life if wished. The choice to go either way is entirely yours. So – What is Yoga? The word YOGA is from the Sanskrit root word "YUJ" which means to join or unite together. In one form or another there is evidence that Yoga has been practiced in India for around 6,000 years. However, the Yoga that is taught in the western world this century is a lot different from that practiced in India hundreds of years ago. This was mostly in a meditation form and only practiced by men until early last century when travelers brought it to the West.

There are many branches of Yoga, the most common is HATHA YOGA, the physical form that, with regular practice, will keep the body exercised, supple and healthy. Along with a good healthy diet and correct amount of rest it can keep even the most sedentary person healthy and fit. Another form of Yoga worth exploring is a light form of RAJA YOGA, where meditation is used more than in Hatha. Although we also practice meditation in Hatha Yoga.

There are eight "LIMBS" of Hatha Yoga. The first two of these, YAMA and NIYAMA, are like a set of rules to live by. They are:-

YAMA
1. Non-destruction

2. Truthfulness

3. Non-stealing

4. Non-desire of possessions of others

5. Moderation in physical pleasures, including eating etc.

NIYAMA
1. Internal and external cleanliness

2. Contentment

3. Strength of character

4. Study

5. Complete self-surrender to the "Spirit"

As Yoga is not a religion, people from all denominations and those with no religious beliefs at all can happily perform Yoga without compromising their beliefs and tenets. However, it is important to remember that in order to successfully live a "Yogic" lifestyle morality should be considered as part of your life. This does not mean you have to live by a strict moral code, but it is important that you care about your fellow living creatures as you do yourself. As the spiritual side of Yoga practice does not infer the existence of a particular God, it is also a good start for someone who has not had a spiritual belief in the past and wishes to explore the possibility that there is "something out there" as that area is approached in meditation. So it is also OK to practice Yoga if you do not believe in a God, Goddess or Higher Being at all.

The remaining six "LIMBS" of Yoga are:

ASANA	Physical movements and postures
PRANAYAMA	Breath control
PRATYAHARA	Control of the nervous system
DHARANA	Mind control

DHYANA	Meditation and contemplation
SAMADHI	Ultimate bliss and spiritual enlightenment
NAMASTE	(The spirit in me acknowledges and respects the spirit in you)

QIGONG

QIGONG is very easy to learn and it is possible to learn this from a video because you are facing the instructor most of the time. There is evidence that people in China were practicing Qigong and Tai Chi over three thousand years ago. Like Yoga, if you practice Qigong or Tai Chi regularly then your health, both physical, mental and emotional can improve as it brings strength and calming to your whole system. There is proof in tests made in China that these practices are beneficial in treating chronic complaints such as hypertension, asthma, arthritis, headaches and a variety of complaints. In recent years Qigong and Tai Chi have come to the West following on the heels of Martial Arts practices. There are also many free classes and groups throughout Australia where you can just go along and learn either or both.

So, who can practice Qigong or Tai Chi? The answer is simple, anyone in some form or another. I learned Qigong about 30 years ago when I had a job that required me to travel and stay in motels for a few days at a time and I found Qigong when I attended a Body Mind and Spirit festival. It can be done in a small room, on a balcony or of course in a park. I use it alongside my Yoga. If you cannot stand for long, or at all, then Qigong can be practiced in a chair, I have taught it to chair bound elderly folk in a local nursing home.

Qigong is also a kind of moving meditation as, once you learn the routine, the mind can close in and just follow the movements. Doing a series of movements repeated over and over is meditative in itself. You should be able to find a simple routine on line or even ask at a local Martial Arts class, they may know of a teacher or class in your area. The easy part of Qigong is that you are facing the teacher, or video, all the time so movements can be easily followed.

The first movement in Qigong, no matter which set of movements are going to be used, is the same. The feet are placed hip distance apart and the knees are relaxed with the arms held loosely by the side of the body leaving a small gap down between the body and the arms, the shoulders are relaxed as is the jaw, the chin slightly down so the eyes are gently downcast. From here the first movement takes place.

Some schools of Qigong also begin by stimulating the Dantien, the area of the body where the Qi (Chee) is 'stored'. This is the energy centre of the body from where the Qi spreads out through the body. It is the area just below the navel, known as the 2nd Chakra in Ayurveda. If a woman or girl places her hands on the Dantien she places her right hand on first with the left over it, a man or boy places his left hand on first then the right over it. Then you relax and concentrate your thoughts on the Dantien. Doing this allows the energy from the Dantien to be released throughout the body. You can move this energy through the body with a simple movement as follows:-

1. With the hands on the Dantien breathe in then slowly bend your knees as you breath out, breathe in then straighten your legs.

2. Separate your hands, palms upward and fingertips pointing towards each other. Hands are kept level with the Dantien.

3. Slowly raise your hands to the chest breathing in and straighten your legs.

4. Turn palms down and lower the hands to the Dantien, breathing out and bending your knees.

5. Turn your hands up once more and repeat the process as often as you like (up to 5 is good).

This is the basic movement of Qigong and can be practiced any time you feel the need. Give it a try.

RETREATS – HEALING OR RELAXATION

You will have seen many ads for retreats and may have been tempted to spend your money and go for a weekend. So, what can you expect to happen? First of all you will probably be interested in one that fits in with what you are currently learning or wish to experience. There are many retreats aimed at spirituality or religion and there are a range of Yoga or healing retreats. The ones aimed at religion will probably be just that. Some are run by different church groups and they will focus on their particular beliefs with prayer time, group discussions etc. However spiritual retreats can be time to spend within your own space in the company of others so you will probably be asked to leave your mobile phone either at home or in their office and you will not be watching TV while you are there. You may be asked to rise very early in the morning for meditation before breakfast and many of them are silent for the majority of the time there. Not the best place for someone like me who talks quite a lot!

However, a weekend of silence is very good for you if you live a busy and noisy life, it gives the mind a chance to reset. Be aware that if the retreat is being run by a Buddhist meditation leader or guru you may be sitting for hours on end in meditation. Yoga retreats are usually run by a well known teacher or Yoga centre and can be set to a program of alternating between Yoga sessions, meditation, quiet time and other gentle physical activity. The food is usually vegetarian. A Healing retreat will often consist of a session with the natural therapist right at the beginning then a program of activities will be tailored to your need. This may consist of massage sessions, sauna or other treatment and the correct food for your healing.

Whatever the retreat is catering for one thing is certain, there will no doubt be very healthy food, quite often vegetarian, alcohol and coffee will be very unlikely and you will usually bunk in with someone else unless you pay a lot of money for a single room. So if you don't like sleeping with strangers perhaps you could take a friend along with you and share a double room. Smoking will definitely be a no no and as I said earlier, the mobile phones will be left at home or in their office. What a good idea! If you are concerned about someone left at home then they will have a phone number you can leave behind so you can be contacted in emergencies.

CRYSTALS

Crystals have many different uses and like many other "new age" ideas they go a very long way back. They were used in ancient times throughout the world to heal, enhance the mind, seek the future and many other ways. A crystal is a very natural stone and should you be offered something that has been tampered with to enhance the colour or brilliance then save your money and go find the real thing. The size of the stone depends on what you want to do with it because a crystal the size of your thumbnail can have the same effect as one the size of your fist. Crystals work by vibrations. Imagine if you can that this piece of rock you are holding is vibrating at a very high rate, you can't see it vibrate but you might feel it. Children can usually feel it and many little ones will pick up a crystal and you can see the reaction on their face. I have had small children tell me that the stone makes them feel nice or not so nice. They are natural.

Physical imbalance can be aided by the wearing of certain crystals and this is especially useful when the body's Chakras are out of alignment. Just the wearing of the correct stone can help this imbalance. Mental imbalance can also be aided. For instance if you are anxious or irritated then having a piece of Amethyst on you can help to calm you. Clear Quartz crystal can be substituted for some other stones and you can be grounded with the use of Obsidian. There are many books available on the use of Crystals. My favourites are the series called Crystal Bible but there is so much information available these days that you may find what you need on line. However, caution once again. Remember, if you have a disease or serious imbalance go and see a professional before treating yourself. It is just as easy to tip the balance the wrong way as it is to heal.

My last word on crystals is this. They can also just look nice as jewellery or ornaments.

THE ANSWER MY FRIEND IS WRITTEN IN THE STARS

SPIRITS, SPIRITUALITY & SPOOKS

There is a big difference between Spirits, Spirituality and Spooks, although they have been known to be lumped together by the ill-informed. So we will take a peek into what the difference is. Let's start with *Spirits*. Now we are not talking about the kind you drink, that is not what this book is all about. We are talking about the kind of Spirits who are spoken to by people who claim to be able to contact the dear departed ie: Dead People. Spirits are elusive because most of us either can't see or hear them or our early religious teachings say they just don't exist. The belief in their existence is something that cannot be forced onto anyone. However, if you do think it is remotely possible that they do exist, then someday you may want to converse with one. So where do you go? Who do you talk to about it? The answer is quite easy, go see a *Medium*. A Medium is a person who has developed a gift they were born with in order to speak to those in the spirit realm – Dead People. The conversation usually takes place after the Medium has meditated for a short while or some other method they have developed. There are many ways the contact can be made. You can spend a small (or large) fortune chasing dead relatives or acquaintances, and that is your choice, or you can go along to a service at one of the many Spiritualist Churches throughout the world. They usually have resident Mediums who, I am told, are very good. And you may end up with a nice cuppa at the end of the service!

However, before you go along to a medium please think of the main reason you need to talk to the Spirit concerned and make sure it is worth the time, energy and possibly money that the procedure will take. Be careful who you hand money over to as most people usually contact a Medium when they are particularly vulnerable from the loss of a loved one and there can be some distress if there is no response from the spirit. The answers you receive could also be contrary to what you expect, so please be prepared for a possible disappointment. Also, not all attempts at contact are successful. After all, you are trying to make contact with a very elusive being. How would you like it if you had recently passed from this mad world into a very peaceful realm and someone keeps upsetting your peace and quiet? I should imagine it would be like trying to watch a very good movie and the telephone keeps ringing. Anyway, just be careful who you approach and how much money you hand over.

And so on to *Spirituality.*

There is a big difference between Spirits and Spirituality. First of all, as you have already read, Spirits are what is within a person or animal and is thought to be left over after a body dies (according to those who believe in this sort of thing as I do). However, spirituality is something a person can experience within themselves. As you have read earlier in this book, we endeavour to reach inside ourselves when meditating to find out about the inner person, or the "self". You also have read a little about reaching out for a higher being, or God. This is the area of spirituality. If you spend time in prayer, talk to either a higher being or the inner self, depending on your beliefs, then this is counted as being "spiritual". Should you believe that there is something about nature that goes beyond the fact that a tree grows, lives and dies then you probably believe that the tree has a "spirit". Whatever you believe in, if this has to do with something beyond the hard fact of materialistic objects then it is possible that you have already a *Spiritual* side to you and you can take this further by either contacting others with similar beliefs or perhaps go on a learning journey yourself to find what it is you are reaching for. This part of your journey into this wonderful new age of learning is purely personal and is your very own private journey. You can share it, but no-one can tell you how to believe. If they do then it is time to put a distance between you and that person. If you can't physically distance yourself then make sure you let them know that their beliefs are not necessarily yours and leave it at that. It doesn't mean you have to shut them out altogether and you can still interact keeping this subject to yourself.

Then there's *SPOOKS*

Depending on your beliefs Spooks could mean ghosts, spirits, poltergeists or many other strange and weird things. I have been asked to "clear" a house that appeared to have a spirit or ghost in it because there were strange noises in the night and windows would bang open by themselves. It was a very old house and after a bit of investigation it turned out that after rain the house would settle itself differently until the ground dried out and things went back to normal. The results of this settling and unsettling were that one of the windows, the old fashioned push open kind, didn't shut properly so the catch gave way and the window flew open, the other noises were merely an old house settling itself in with it's creaks and groans (a bit like we do when we get old!). I am not a builder but on my advice the house owner did ask a builder about it and it confirmed my suggestion. Spirits are another matter altogether. A dear friend of mine had rented an old house on a property in the Scenic Rim area of Queensland. Her two children in their pre-teens, who both slept in the same room, had told her they were visited in the night by two children. Now my friend's children were not too surprised by this because they came from a spiritually aware family and they actually thought it was "cool" that they had these visits. However it became a bit too much to deal with when the spirit children started rocking the beds at night – so I was asked if I could do anything. We did some digging and found out that over 100 years before there was a massive flood in the area. The father of the children had left them at home and taken his row boat to pick up their mother in the nearby town. He didn't mean to leave them long but the flood became a torrent and he couldn't get back to the house. Thinking the children would be safe in the house he waited until the next day when the water receded and, with his wife, went home to find that the water had inundated the house and the poor children had drowned. The adults left the house and made their life elsewhere. However, the spirits of the children had remained and could not leave. Knowing this I was able, with the help of another beautiful soul, to send the children's spirits on their way. I will not go into how this was done but it was peaceful afterwards.

POLTERGEISTS and other temperamental beasties

I don't know anything about Poltergeists apart from the fact that if you have one in your house or building you should make sure that you can duck quickly. I have heard of objects being thrown across the room or being knocked over so I do believe they exist but haven't had the 'pleasure' of experiencing it myself. If you think you have such a creature then you probably need to find someone who can reason with them before they wreck your house. I do believe they are restless spirits who have become frustrated that they cannot move on so most likely a good spiritualist could talk some sense into them and ask them to move on.

So, on the matter of moving spirits on who are stuck in your house, make sure you are nice to them because they are probably not there by choice. A vase of flowers or a plant pot in flower near an open window is often a nice gesture then ask the spirit to leave in peace – nicely – and if you think you are successful then a good smudging with White Sage is probably your next move. Good luck. Or, find a good spiritualist who comes recommended by a friend. Smudging is done by either lighting a couple of incense sticks or a bundle of herbs and using the smoke to cleanse the space. Make sure you are fire safe by holding the burning herbs or incense over a bowl or dish so none of the ash drops onto the floor. You then proceed to walk around the room, especially into corners and allow the smoke to waft around. I like to do this with all doors and windows open to allow any bad energy to leave and of course it helps the spirits move on. They need to be out in the open air in order to pass on to the next stage. Once you have done this smudging and you feel the room is clear then you can close the windows etc. I would then place fresh flowers in the room for a couple of days. And throughout all this please remove or unplug from the wall any electronics – we still are not sure if emitted waves etc can cause a room to become blocked. If you are still in doubt please get a copy of GHOST WRITER by my friend J.L. Addicoat!

RUNES, TAROT CARDS AND PALMISTRY

For thousands of years there have been people who need to find out what is happening outside their daily lives, either to find out why something is happening in their lives, has happened or is going to happen. Consulting a clairvoyant, clairaudient, tarot reader, palm reader or the runes goes back so far in time that it probably existed with the cave people. So, is there anything in it? Well yes there is. The Tarot cards are many and varied as are the people who are able to interpret them. Many people have their own cards and will do a spread on a daily basis or when the need arises to discover if something is changing in their lives and others will go to a Reader who will do it for them. The cards are usually laid out after shuffling by the person needing the reading so their energy is transferred to the cards.

Once the cards are laid out then the reader will interpret the spread. Some money usually changes hands with the premise that there is a value placed on the opinion of the reader by the client. A Clairvoyant on the other hand usually does not need cards but may use some other item such as crystals to "connect" with the client then after spending moments connecting with spirit a reading may come to hand. A Clairaudient is similar but will often 'hear' or feel words from the spirit of either the client or some other being that enables them to give the client information relevant to questions being asked. Sometimes smells or sounds will be interpreted as part of the reading. If you have decided to have such a reading done please remember that like many other things there are charlatans about that will take your money and make up stories. However, there are many talented folk who are genuine. It is very hard to distinguish one from the other except that the best result is from the person to whom you did not give out too much information to start with. If you are asked too many questions in the beginning then you are probably going to fork out money for information that has been gleaned from that information you handed over without thinking. I cannot explain my ability to know things about a client that has not been given to me but I can. I usually ask for something that the client wears, such as a watch, ring or necklace that has come into contact with their person because this holds their energy and it is the link that I require. I am often asked to find some lost item for a friend and most of the time it works but of course there are always mischievous beings about who will feed me false information or lead me on a wild goose chase! That is the way of the Universe.

Palmistry is the reading of the lines on the hand and is also a very old method of determining someone's life. The lines, supposedly, can give you an idea of your health, length of life, how many children you might have, what you might end up doing for a living and many other interesting things. The lines on your hands do reflect your life and a good reader will take the right hand differently to the left. It can be a bit of fun too.

Runes have been around since before the Roman Empire as it was through Runes that the Druids and their predecessors were able to predict what was happening. The most common seem to be the Runes of the Scandinavian countries and it is usually these that are used most of the time. Basically the rune stones are marked with the runic symbols and when they are chosen randomly can be interpreted to answer a question. There are many books on the subject and if you want to have your own rune stones then you will probably get a book with them that will interpret your selection.

Like all "fortune telling" please remember that it is not an exact science and there are many different ways of reading either the cards, the runes or the stones. Ask the questions but please do not rely on the answers to rule your life. Allow your life to flow on, see it as a challenge with results that can be either positive or negative. Life is an adventure that we have one shot at so if we constantly want answers in order to make daily decisions then all you will end up with is anxiety when the answers are not what we really wanted in the first place.

MAGIC AND WHERE TO FIND IT

Sometimes the day goes by completely without any magic happening, on other days there seems to be magic in the air all day – can you see it or feel it?

Magic can come from so many different directions and have so many different effects on people – is it any wonder that many people don't even notice it.

Take ducks for instance!! Ducks you say, why ducks? Have you ever driven around the corner on your way to work, thinking of all the mundane things you have to do in order to earn your bread and butter, then out of the blue there they are – ducks – a whole family of them. Strutting along behind mum is a little row of ducklings with dad bringing up the rear. They are just waddling along to wherever it is they are headed to find breakfast, quite oblivious of the world around them. Have you ever just stopped and watched them? I have. It was one morning when I was a little early for work after dropping my beloved off at his work while his car was being serviced. I pulled in at a local lake with a beautiful park between it and the road and walked down towards the water – just for a bit of fresh air. As I came to the water this little family of ducklings swam away from the edge where I was standing. I hadn't even seen them there at first but they saw me. They didn't go far initially then it was as if the leader spotted a nice feast and headed for the bank further up, of course everyone else followed the leader. Next thing that happened was that mum (or dad I couldn't tell) came swimming past me, up the bank, rounded up the kids and herded them back into the water. A little magic for the day.

As I have a beautiful garden we have a lot of creatures visit us. Another magic event was the day I was sitting having a coffee when a beautiful green snake poked his head up, slithered down into the water in the pond and began to search for food. A few minutes later another one, same colour, same size, came from another bush and headed for the water also at a different spot. These snakes are harmless and inhabit our garden, they have their families somewhere in the ferns and raise their children to just keep a respectable distance from us. As does the large carpet snake who inhabits the roof during winter. The birds treat us to magic events all the time and occasionally so do the plants.

My magic is "earth magic", it doesn't come from a magic wand or an earthly magician, it comes from the spirits around me.

The other kind of magic is that created by the humans around me. My beautiful partner creates magic for me by his presence, my children and grandchildren astound me with their love and magic. Especially the grandchildren when they were small. Have you ever sat and watched your children or grandchildren play – totally oblivious of your presence or drawing you into their magical lives to share their magic. If you haven't then you have been missing out on the most profound magic. Try it.

Of course when most of us think of magic we think of the kind that is conjured up by a very special person with a wand or other props. That magic is good too because it makes us think outside our normal boundaries of thought – something we should all do now and then. What a pity that some magicians seem to need to make fools of people to get their point across. Wouldn't it be much nicer if they created magic to make their "subjects" feel good? However, the world is made up of the good the bad and the plain outright ignorant so we won't give them energy by talking about them. I did enjoy Harry Potter though.

I have friends who practice Candle Magic and other treasures of Wicca. These lovely people send their magic to those they love and care for in order to better the lives of those beloved. Such a pity that most people misunderstand this type of magic, for it is only done for the good of all. Of course there will always be those who practise the art of Black Magic. I prefer not to discuss this in detail, however, like everything else in the Universe there needs to be always a balance of energies and although there are some who practise Black Magic for evil there are also many who do so for need. The image of a person in a long black cloak holding onto a skull and murmuring strange words comes to mind for some. However, many who practise this art look like ordinary people, but they choose their path and will always be aware of the consequences of their actions just like those who practise White Magic.

So, getting back to magic. If you want to play with spells and other incantations please remember, the Universe does listen so be careful what you ask for. Creating a spell to attract that good looking person in the coffee shop may turn into a nightmare when you discover that not only are they good looking but when they leave work and go home they do so to a family of their own and the spell you created might cause havoc in their lives. However the Law of Attraction can be used by making a list of the traits you would like in a new partner and a list of the ones you would not like. No names or personal details should go into this. Once you have written down this list put it somewhere where it won't be touched by anyone else or somewhere you consider special and silently ask the Universe to find that person for you. Leave it there and be patient because sometimes it takes a bit of time for the Universe to find this special person. Remember, once more, be careful what you ask for and make sure the things you don't want in a person are also noted as such. You don't want to attract someone with nasty controlling traits do you?

FAIRIES, ELVES AND OTHER CREATURES

Fairy magic is, of course, the best of all. If you haven't experienced this since childhood then I suggest you go and ask a child (if you haven't got one of your own make sure their parents say it's OK first though), then ask them to *teach you* something for a change. Children love to be asked to teach an adult something of their world. Go ahead, ask one!! However, in order to get the real fairy magic story you might have to find a child who isn't constantly staring at a computer or TV. Now that's the real challenge, finding one. Off you go then. Of course, if you, like me, still believe in the fairy folk (or faerie as we usually refer to them) then you know all about this subject and need to take it no further, however you might like to hear my take on the subject. Please don't forget the fairies that live in your home, the ones that hide things from you then return them to the very same place a few days later. They are the ones who hang around the men of the family. (Sorry – can't help myself there).

In nearly every culture around the world there are magical creatures of some kind in their folklore. The Irish have the 'Little folk' as do the Scots and many others. In Australia there are many stories in the Dreamtime that talk of such creatures as do the old stories from many lands. Over the past couple of thousand years our so-called sophisticated upbringing has gradually removed these wonderful stories from many societies. Luckily I was brought up in a family that embraced such stories. My Scottish father would talk of the Wee Folk and as my sister and I were introduced to Brownies as soon as we were old enough there were elves and fairies in abundance. Thankfully we are now seeing an emergence of folk who are exploring this wonderful culture. So go and find your magic. Spend time in nature, that's the best place to find them. If you were brought up with such stories and think that it is not the thing for an adult, think again. Tolkien brought them back to life in the Lord of The Rings and Hobbit books and movies and if you have seen any of these then think of the Elves. Everything is possible. To attract these magical folk into your life then you need to remove danger from your home and garden, such as poisons and non-natural plant foods. Leaving a treat like a small piece of cake or honey out on the night of a full moon may be all that is needed if they are about. Come out in the morning and see that the treat has gone – was it an animal or a fairy? Who can tell. However, the possibility is there is it not. And remember, next time you can't find something for a few days then it turns up – well, if nothing else it gives you a reason for not seeing it in the first place!!!!

The best way to begin is to read books about fairies etc. Borrow the kids' books if necessary and if you are looking through these in the library you can always pretend you are going to talk to children about the fairies can't you? If you get an opportunity to dress up in "magical" costume for a party or other occasion then go for it. They don't mind being copied, in fact they take it as a compliment. Thankfully there has been a resurgence of a belief in the land of faerie over the past few decades, although I believe it never really went away it was just not spoken of. We have built a small garden for the fairies and a bigger one for the gnomes and elves. It gives us great pleasure to sit and look at these little pockets of fantasy and although the inhabitants (during the day) are made of plaster and concrete the surroundings have been put there with the intention that if we do have the real folk then they are welcome to spend time there. Maybe they will see this as their fantasy land! If, sadly, these magical creatures disappeared from your life once you reached puberty then perhaps you would like to try and find them again. Maybe you have been brought up with a belief in Angels or you have discovered them through poking around in the realm of Angel readings. If you haven't seen an Angel in the flesh does that mean you, or many other people, do not believe in their existence? If you were brought up in some Christian religions then Angels are probably within those teachings. So, think about that, if you can believe in an invisible human size Angel, why not in a tiny – or not - fairy? I'll leave you with that one.

DRUIDS AND PAGANS IN THE MODERN WORLD

Before you continue to read this chapter I would like to state that following Druidism, Paganism, Witchcraft and Wicca are not all the same thing. There are many practices that cross over from one to the other, however, not all Pagans are Wiccans and not all Pagans are Witches although most witches or Wiccans would consider themselves pagan. During the past 2,000 years there have been so many instances where Paganism was considered to be Witchcraft and when Crowley developed the modern version of Witchcraft and called it Wicca then it was considered by many that Paganism was the same thing. It is not. There are many Pagans and Druids who have nothing to do with magic and base their beliefs on the energies surrounding this wonderful planet of ours. They worship the Earth because it is the Earth that provides most of the things that keep us alive. They worship the sun because of it's power and respect the other elements of Water, Air and Ether for similar reasons not because it is considered a god. Giving thanks to these elements at different times of the year is the same as a Christian giving thanks to their God for providing the necessities of life and is not too far from a child thanking their parent for providing sustenance. If you have witnessed a Pagan or Druid ritual you will have seen the participants holding hands to the sun or the moon and giving thanks. There is usually no priest or priestess involved, perhaps only someone who leads the ritual and that is usually someone from the local community who may have the knowledge required. However, to become a Druid you will be asked to learn many things that are based on natural energies and although many may take part in Druid rituals there is usually a very learned person, called a Druid, who has studied for many, sometimes 10 or more, years to have that knowledge. In days gone past this was never written down but taught verbally. The Romans saw the Druids in Britain and other parts of Europe as a threat to their superiority because many folk throughout Europe and Britain followed the Druid teachings. The Romans, as was their way, denounced the Druids because they saw them as a threat to their strength as rulers and forced them into hiding. However they let the common folk still worship their seasons and, as they did later on when Rome converted to Christianity, blended the old gods and goddesses with the Christian version where possible. And so they manipulated the Goddess into being worshipped as the Virgin Mary and some of the other higher beings became some of the early saints. A good example is Brigid who was an important part of Irish mythology and later on was worshipped as St Brigid. You may even find, if you travel overseas, that there are many societies that practise both Earth based beliefs as well as Christianity or another organised religion and that is quite acceptable to them.

So, please do not think that Pagans and Druids are witches because, although some might be, most are not.

There has also been a resurgence of Shamanism in recent times. So what is a Shaman. First of all the plural of Shaman is Shamans. Just in case you needed to know that. Now on with the important stuff. A Shaman takes many years in training and the connection to the Earth and other elements is the basis of their beliefs. They do perform what some might call magic and this is why there seems to be so much mysticism involved. The use of a drum to keep a constant rhythm is important and will often be used to enter a trance like state. Certain tempos create brainwaves that allow one to enter a theta state and allows Spirit travelling. The beat of the drum can also imitate the beating heart of the Earth Mother. The use of plants, precious stones are also used. You will have, no doubt, seen images of a Shaman in North America or Mongolia dancing and drumming and there are still many places where they are called upon to assist the dying to move on into the next realm. Sometimes the chanting is in a language that is unknown as some of the chants go back to a time where different languages were used by the spirit workers. Please do not think you can go out and do a 2 week course and come back as a Shaman. There are many years of training and many spirit journeys involved and even then a Shaman will always be learning.

Most of the Pagan information that is generally available is set in the Northern Hemisphere. The Sabbaths and celebrations are totally opposite what is required in Australia so I am including a list of these with dates appropriate for the southern hemisphere.

TRADITIONAL PAGAN CELEBRATIONS FOR THE SOUTHERN HEMISPHERE

The seasons are celebrated in the same way but the dates are opposite according to our southern seasons. As Yule or Winter Solstice is the traditional start of the year I will begin there.

WINTER SOLSTICE - June 21 (approximately) or longest night of the year

In many parts of Australia this is the coldest time of the year and as such celebrations can be similar to those in the Northern Hemisphere with the sorts of food and drink associated with traditional Christmas such as fruit cake, fruit mince pies, egg nog and mulled wine. In the northern parts it is the period of the "dry" when it is good to sit outside around a fire telling stories or just enjoying company. The night sky throughout Australia is clear at this time of year with Sagittarius and Corona Australis rising in the East and the Milky Way is in full view. In nature there is only one native deciduous tree, that is a Beech that grows in Tasmania and it will lose its leaves at this time of the year. Many native trees are flowering, especially the wattle and in the north cassowaries are laying eggs and white cockatoo chickens are hatching. Some aboriginal folk watched the return of the whales into the warmer waters with their calves to enjoy the sea grasses that grow at this time of year. Life beginning once again.

To celebrate this season you could light a fire outside in a fire pit or even in your fireplace if you have one. If you can't have a fire then perhaps some candles (safely please) in a cluster on a tray would be a good substitute, even a torch covered in red cellophane would be a last resort but safer than candles indoors. Sit around the fire and talk to each other. Shutting off all technology for the night and return to the way stories were always passed around, verbally. Invite friends and/or relatives around and enjoy food that is associated with Christmas time as this is a celebration. In the morning greet the sun and give thanks for the new day and the beginning of the new year.

IMBOLC – August 1

Imbolc marks the end of winter and the beginning of Spring. Although we usually recognise the beginning of Spring by the calendar as 1st September. A time when greenery begins to appear and warmer climate seeds can be sown. Known as Oimele, meaning 'sheeps milk' is a time when ewes begin to produce milk. The celebration is sacred to the Irish Goddess Brigid. I will not dwell on this part of the celebration. In Australian the weather alternates between cold and hot and there is much abundance as baby birds emerge and plant life almost explodes. In Queensland the cold winds can come blustering in from the west and the warmer breezes come from the Pacific ocean. It is a time of change and a time to celebrate those changes.

EOSTRE – September 22

This is one of the celebrations that has become mixed up with the Christian Easter in the northern hemisphere. However, it predates Christianity and is a time of abundance. It is a time of new life and is celebrated as such. The Hare used to be associated with this time because it was a symbol of fertility. (Easter Bunny anyone) In Australian north it is a time when the weather begins to become humid with vigorous plant growth. However, in other places it is hot and dry and the waterholes begin to dry up. Prior to this the long dry grasses were traditionally burnt to make way for the new growth and thankfully this is once again being practiced. It is a time of change also in the south where snow will be melting and animals that have been hiding from the cold will emerge.

Celebrate this season by planting seeds, mowing long grass that doesn't need to be where it is and tidy up before the spring storms arrive.

BELTANE – November 1

Beltane means 'Bright Fire' and signifies the beginning of Summer (according to tradition not the calendar). Traditionally, on the eve of this festival all household fires were extinguished and the next morning a huge bonfire was erected. Once the fire was lit people jumped over this fire for blessing and protection then took coals home to rekindle their household fires. This is the celebration that gave birth to the maypole and many other festival ideas and traditions that do not seem so important in the southern hemisphere so it is a time to honour new and more appropriate celebrations. First of all lighting fires outside in many parts of Australia is unwise and illegal at this time of year so please consider this when you are looking to celebrate Beltane. I have personally been to a Beltane celebration where the "fire" was a pile of logs with a torch in the centre and red cellophane over the top. We jumped over that and it was just as potent because the intent was there.

In Australia there are many changes at this time of year. In the north the sky is becoming gloomy as the rainy season works itself up and storms begin. There are often hints of Cyclones in the far north and people begin to batten down for the coming storms. The rest of Australia is so varied that one celebration that might suit folks in Melbourne will not be appropriate in Darwin. The best way to celebrate Beltane is to honour the season in your own area and get together with friends for a Barbeque. What better way to celebrate the coming of summer. Go for a walk in the bush or on the beach, walk on the Earth barefoot if you can safely and, if you are in a secure place away from prying eyes, fling off your clothes and let the sun warm your naked body – but only for 10 minutes you don't want to get sunburn.

LITHA – Summer Solstice - 22 December

(or thereabouts)

This is the celebration of Mid Summer and where we celebrated the longest night in June we celebrate the shortest night on this day. It is also the celebration of the waning of the sun so the Sun God, if you like, begins to become more potent as if trying to ward off the reduction of its power. The celebrations were traditionally celebrated around fire in the form of bonfires, fire wheels and torches but of course this is highly inappropriate in Australia at this time of year. However as this is the time of celebrations in Australia then we are already in a festive mood.

One great tradition that can be practiced at this time of year is communication with the fairies, the little people, the spirits and others from that amazing magical realm. Leave cake and milk out at night to attract them (although we all know it will be the normal night creatures who will take it). Encourage the spirits and fairies with bunches of flowers strewn about the place and make them welcome.

If you want to celebrate this season as Litha there is a lot of information available on how you can do this.

LUGHNASAD – February 1

Traditionally this is the season of the first harvest. It is too early in Australia to be thinking of this and outside the cities it is probably not celebrated at all. In the north there are cyclones or storms and much of Australia suffers from floods or bush fires. However, there are always positives. Gather together friends and celebrate life, look after those who have been affected by such natural disasters, volunteer with the bush fire brigade or the SES or just ask about to see if anyone is in trouble from flood, storm or fire. Be caring or just do what you can.

MABON – Autumn Equinox - March 22

This is the season of thanksgiving. A time of harvest – even in Australia – and the celebrations are around food with the storing of food for winter and a time of production for farmers. In recent times of drought it was also, sadly, a time when many had to leave their land to try something else. This was also a new beginning of sorts although it can also be a time of heartbreak. If you would like to celebrate Mabon then do it by honoring the folk who grow the food, the earth that produces it and give thanks to whoever you believe in for any bounty there is. However, on the good side it is the beginning of the end of the Monsoon in the north and the receding of flood waters. The risk of bush fires is diminishing and the busy emergency services can take a breath. In northern Indigenous culture an orange or red sunset tells the people that the dry season is on its way.

Celebrate with friends and relatives with things associated with harvest. Fresh baked bread, lots of fruit and vegetables and other food that is natural. If you wish to celebrate in a more 'Pagan' way there is a lot of information available.

SAMHAIN – May 1

This is the celebration many people have heard of as with Beltane. Traditionally it was a time to plant the next crop, slaughter animals to be smoked or preserved for the cold of winter. However, in modern times it is not necessary for this part. However, the animals can still be honored and blessed.

Offerings were made to the fairy folk at this time of year for protection during winter. There are many other traditions connected with Samhain including honoring the dead but I will not go into them here. If you wish to look into this then there is plenty of information available.

In Australia the weather starts to cool down in the south and become very pleasant in the north. Winter crops are planted and some trees give out a burst of colour before becoming dormant. Celebrate by planting some winter growing crops or clearing up the summer growth. Get together with friends and make preserves, jams, sauces and prepare herbs for drying. Tell loving stories about loved ones that have passed over and honour their memories with the good things you remember about them not the sadness.

Much of this information I have gleaned from a wonderful book called **Practicing The Witch's Craft. Real magic under a southern sky. By Douglas Ezzy.** The book contains input from many other people and I have found it invaluable for information on being a Pagan in the southern hemisphere.

Just remember, celebrating the seasons is not about witchcraft or Wicca, it is about traditions that go well beyond organised religions and, until not that many decades ago, was passed down verbally and through community. Enjoy the seasons in your own area and make your own traditions that you can pass on to your children and beyond.

Before going on to the next chapter I would like to mention something important about the folk we call Witches. There are many different views on what it a witch. Somewhere along the way Wise Women, Herbalists and Healers were classed by authorities as Witches. Some may have been, however, most were not. The old woman in the village was more likely to be the person you went to just like you would go to the doctor or naturopath today. She would give you a herbal mixture to take and most of the time it would heal your problem. There were those who practised energy healing, much like a Reiki healer today. A Wise Woman would be the midwife, herbalist and counsellor and she would have trained for many years from girlhood under another Wise Woman. So please remember, not all witches sit around a cauldron saying "Hubble bubble toil and trouble". That one was invented by Shakespeare.

LEARNING MORE

There is so much to learn and you will probably want to extend your knowledge as soon as you can, but wait, there's more! You have a lifetime to learn and that is really what this "New Age" is all about. We have crossed over into an era where the spiritual and mental health of a person is as important as the physical health. We have finally realised that there is no point in having millions in the bank if your body can't keep up with your lifestyle or your mind has taken you out of it. Once it was nice to have a "dotty" aunt or an uncle who had gone off to Africa to find him or her self. But then things changed, and those aunts and uncles were classed as psychotic or deranged and were put on medication to make them conform to society's ideal of normal. The same thing has happened to children who are "not quite normal". Drugs and Counsellors have become the place to go if our little one talks to imaginative friends after the age of 5. Our minds have been played with over the last several decades and it became socially unacceptable to be a bit strange. Well, not any more. You can be dotty again so long as you're not dangerous and people will actually think you are wonderful for it.

How do you rate yourself in the sanity department? If you are considered "normal" by society, does this mean you are? I would like to think people did not class me in that category because that would put me in the same category as lots of other people, and I don't think I am. Are you? So what is normal? Not being a psychiatrist (I even have trouble spelling it), I would consider normal to be someone who goes about his or her daily habits unnoticed by the rest of the human race. In order to make an impression on others or themselves they would need to do something extra special either at work or perhaps playing sport, music or some other achievement in their chosen field. And there is nothing wrong with being classed as "normal". However, what if you don't fit into this classification?

You have picked up this book, you have read up to this paragraph and you are still reading. This may possibly mean that you are getting something out of it, and I really hope you are. Guess what, you have passed out of "normal" and are now in the free thinking, free acting "new age" society. Congratulations, you have crossed out of the comfort zone and made your own way. Watch out – according to some people you may be getting dangerously close to becoming eccentric, dotty or even close to becoming a modern day hippy. How wonderful. Now you may even be found wandering around markets, shopping for clothes where they sell cheesecloth shirts or in op shops, wearing beads and even going outside at night to look up at the moon and stars. What will it be next – talking to trees? I hope so.

Thank you for spending this time wandering through the wonderful ideas I have collected in my many years in this life on this earth at this time in history. It is wonderful to now be the "dotty aunt" I admired in two of mine many, many years ago. I believe it is a wonderful fulfilment of life's teachings to be able to pass mine on to you. And I thank you for joining me on the journey.

Namaste

ABOUT THE AUTHOR

Living in a quiet Eco Village in Central Queensland, Australia with husband and best friend Rob has given Heather the time and energy to follow up on ideas that have been in the melting pot for many years. As a Freelance Journalist there was the satisfaction of letting readers know what was happening, however her storytelling gift finally surfaced with the release of Under Her Protection in 2020 followed by Finding Bicycles the following year. Moving away from fiction for a while this new adventure has given her the opportunity to share with her readers all the wonderful information she has gleaned during the several decades she has been in this life at this time in history.

BY THE SAME AUTHOR

UNDER HER PROTECTION – Published 2020

In a future following the Climate Catastrophe that changed the Earth forever, a gang of marauders are terrorising the people on the Plains of Parlat. Nothing has been able to stop them until a local Wise Woman decides enough is enough and with the help of others sets about to be rid of them once and for all. Good natural magic and a bit of help from a surprising source finally solves the problem.

FINDING BICYCLES – Published 2021

In a future many years following the collapse of the technical age and a return of many societies to the simple ways of the Middle Ages, Rosalind will tell you the story as she lives her life between being a member of a community of women who follow the ways of the Earth Mother and the avid traveler seeing the world with her father. From a rather precarious event as a young girl on her way to be married to learning the ways to heal and teach nature's ways she occasionally escapes to the high seas with her father and discovers that not all the world has lost the technology and lifestyles that she believed disappeared with the Great Climate Catastrophe.

www.ingramcontent.com/pod-product-compliance
Lightning Source LLC
Chambersburg PA
CBHW070306010526
44107CB00056B/2501